p42 Pear + Rice Salad

THE BIG BROCCOLI BOOK

THE
BIG
CARROT
BOOK

THE
BIG
CARROT
BOOK

....

GEORGIA DOWNARD

RANDOM HOUSE NEW YORK

Library of Congress Cataloging-in-Publication Data
Downard, Georgia.
The big carrot book / Georgia Downard. — 1st ed.
p.   cm.
Includes index.
ISBN 0-679-43824-6
1. Cookery (Carrots)   I. Title.
TX803.C35D69   1995
641.6'513—dc20   95-14768

Manufactured in the United States of America on acid-free paper
24689753
First Edition

Illustrations and book design by Lilly Langotsky

FOR MARIE HAAS,

WHO ADDS NEW DIMENSION TO THE MEANING

OF THE WORD "FRIEND"

The time is coming when a single carrot, freshly observed, will set off a revolution.

—Joachim Gasquet, *Paul Cézanne*

"Shucks," said the bunny, "I might just as well stay where I am and be your little bunny."

And so he did.
"Have a carrot," said the mother bunny.

—Margaret Wise Brown, *The Runaway Bunny*

ACKNOWLEDGMENTS

• •

I would like to thank Tina, Elizabeth, Lauren, Cathy, Melissa, and Segal for their invaluable assistance.

I would also like to thank Lawrence LaRose for his patience and help in bringing this book to fruition; Jean-Isabel McNutt for her expert copyediting; and Lilly Langotsky for her beautiful drawings.

CONTENTS

....

SALADS

ENTRÉES

SIDE DISHES

BREADS

DESSERTS

INDEX

THE
BIG
CARROT
BOOK

A WORD ABOUT CARROTS

Perhaps because they are considered a "staple" vegetable—available year round, inexpensive, and, if stored properly, relatively long-lasting—most people view carrots with little interest and even less enthusiasm. Yet carrots are one of the most versatile members of the vegetable family. Traditionally relegated to side dishes or included in savory entrées, carrots work equally well in breads, muffins, and desserts. Appropriate for both formal or informal meals, carrots are easily adapted to different occasions. For instance, when paired with fresh spices, grated citrus peel, and a good chicken broth, a soup made from carrots easily competes with an expensive seafood bisque or rich consommé as the first course in an elegant meal. And yet what could be simpler or more satisfying than a quick carrot sauté, particularly on the holiday table? Served uncooked in salads and as hors d'oeuvres they impart a sweet crispness that is both refreshing and unique.

Jane Grigson points out in her masterful *Vegetable Book* that carrots were once highly prized both as an exotic food and delicate ornament: "Ladies of the Stuart court pinned the young feathery plumage of young carrots to their heads and on their splendid hats."*

The Vegetable Book, Jane Grigson, Atheneum (New York 1979), p. 160.

Unlike the bright orange variety most familiar in this country, early carrots derived from a purple species first grown in Afghanistan during the early seventh century. Seeds from purple carrots, together with a yellow mutant variety, were brought by the Moors to Western Europe. In the Middle Ages, the Dutch produced the bright orange carrot we know today. During Colonial times the roots were carried to America by early English settlers, and by the nineteenth century, carrots were a staple vegetable in both Europe and America.

Today most cultivated carrots are orange and have long, tapered roots, yet there are round-shaped varieties resembling large raddishes, as well as red, white, purple, black and yellow ones. Some of the newest carrot varieties are bred to have a high beta-carotene content. Supercarrots, such as Juwarot and Beta III, contain from 40 to 70 percent more beta-carotene than ordinary carrots.

The interest in producing carrots high in beta-carotene results from recent studies showing carrots to be a natural source of this antioxidant. Beta-carotene is a deep-orange compound abundant in carrots, sweet potatoes, and cantaloupes. The body converts beta-carotene into Vitamin A. While a person can overdose on the Vitamin A found in nutritional supplements (which the body stores in the liver), naturally occurring beta-carotene is nontoxic even in large amounts. Once eaten, it is stored in skin tissue and body fat until needed, at which time it is converted into Vitamin A. Eating carrots is one of the best and most natural ways to include the recommended daily allowance of Vitamin A and beta-carotene in your diet. One carrot a day can provide enough Vitamin A to meet the FDA's recommended daily allowance. The populations of countries such as Japan and Norway, where diets are rich in beta-carotene, have low incidences of lung, colon, prostate, cervical, and breast cancer. In addition, Vitamin A improves our ability to see in dim light and can aid in preventing night blindness—adding some credence to the belief that eating carrots improves eyesight. It is also important in the maintenance of healthy skin.

BUYING

· · · · · · · · · · ·

When purchasing carrots, look for crisp, bright orange roots with smooth, satiny skin and healthy green tops. Avoid carrots that are "dusty" in appearance or split—an indication not only of age but of improper storing. Also, feathery roots running along the length of the carrot and sprouting tops are indications of maturity and improper handling.

Don't be fooled by the orange-tinted bags that many distributors use. Be sure to examine the carrots through clear plastic or by taking them out of the bag.

STORING

· · · · · · · · · · · ·

Remove the green tops and place the carrots in a perforated plastic bag in the refrigerator. They will keep for up to two weeks.

COOKING

· · · · · · · · · · · · · · ·

Young fresh carrots need not be peeled. Simply scrub them with a vegetable brush and trim their tops. Older, larger carrots, which are ideal for soups and stews, need to be peeled and their woody interiors removed and discarded.

There are various methods for cooking carrots. They may be combined with cold salted water, a little butter and a pinch of sugar, brought to a boil and simmered, covered, until tender. Alternatively, they may be steamed, stir-fried, or roasted. Whatever method you employ, the most important consideration is that they not be overcooked. They are best eaten when their texture as well as their color is retained.

A NOTE ON THE RECIPES

· ·

As I mentioned in *The Big Broccoli Book,* substitutions may be made for those who are watching their intake of fats and cholesterol. Low-fat milk may be substituted for cream. The addition of milk or cream may be eliminated altogether when making soups. Plain yogurt may be substituted for sour cream, and olive, canola, or vegetable oil for butter and margarine.

In developing the recipes for this book I have come to respect this wonderful vegetable, and will no longer take carrots for granted. Perhaps if carrots were only seasonally available, and, therefore, quite expensive, we would appreciate them for their true worth. The versatility of carrots is quite astounding. Instead of exhausting the subject I have simply touched upon it. I can only hope these recipes will whet your appetite and change any preconceived ideas you may have had concerning the "plebian" reputation of carrots, finally giving them their proper accord in the hierarchy of vegetables. Use these recipes as a springboard for creating your own.

SOUPS

GINGERED CARROT SOUP

Carrots and ginger seem to have an affinity for each other. This soup makes a wonderful light lunch when served with a fresh green salad and warm biscuits.

3 tablespoons butter
1 cup minced onion
1 pound carrots, peeled and
*   sliced*
1 small rib celery, sliced
1 tablespoon minced fresh
*   gingerroot*

3 tablespoons flour
5 cups chicken stock or broth
½ teaspoon grated lemon peel
1 bay leaf
1 teaspoon sugar
Salt
Pepper

In a large saucepan, melt the butter over moderately low heat, add the onion, carrots, celery, and ginger, and cook, covered, stirring occasionally, for 8 minutes. Add the flour and cook, stirring, for 2 more minutes. Add stock, lemon peel, bay leaf, sugar, and salt and pepper to taste. Simmer the soup, covered, for 45 minutes, or until the carrots are very tender. Discard the bay leaf.

Puree the soup in batches in a food processor or blender, return to the saucepan, and simmer, stirring, until heated through. Makes 6 cups, serving 4.

CARROT, LEEK, AND POTATO SOUP

This soup may be served hot or cold. When chilled, it is a new twist on the classic vichyssoise. Remember to increase the seasoning in the soup if serving cold.

3 tablespoons unsalted butter
2 cups minced leeks (white part only)
1 ½ pounds carrots, peeled and sliced
½ pound boiling potatoes, peeled and cubed
5 cups chicken stock or broth

1 sprig fresh thyme or 1 teaspoon dried
1 bay leaf
Salt
White pepper
1 cup light cream or milk
Sour cream for garnish

In a large saucepan, melt the butter over moderately low heat, add the leeks, carrots, and potatoes and cook, covered, stirring occasionally, for 5 minutes. Add the stock, thyme, bay leaf, and salt and pepper to taste. Simmer, covered, for 45 minutes, or until the carrots are very tender. Discard the thyme and bay leaf.

Puree the soup in batches in a food processor or blender, and return to the saucepan. Stir in the cream and simmer the soup, stirring, until it is heated through. Garnish with the sour cream. If serving chilled, refrigerate the soup, covered, for at least 2 hours or overnight. Stir the soup before serving, adjust the seasoning, and garnish with the sour cream. Makes about 9 cups, serving 6.

ICED CARROT AND ORANGE SOUP

This refreshing soup is particularly appealing during the dog days of August. Garnish it with Dilled Yogurt Cream (p. 27) and homemade croutons.

3 tablespoons unsalted butter
½ cup minced shallots
1 pound carrots, peeled and
  sliced
3 cups chicken broth

1 teaspoon grated orange peel
Salt
2 cups orange juice
Dilled Yogurt Cream for garnish
  (p. 27)

In a large saucepan, melt the butter over moderately low heat. Cook the shallots and carrots, covered, stirring occasionally, for 5 minutes. Add the broth, orange peel and salt to taste. Simmer, covered, stirring occasionally, for 45 minutes, or until the carrots are very tender.

Puree the carrot mixture in batches in a food processor or blender, and transfer to a bowl. Let cool and chill, covered, for at least 1 hour. Stir in the orange juice, adding more salt to taste, and ladle the soup into bowls. Garnish with the Dilled Yogurt Cream. Makes about 6 cups, serving 4.

CREAMY CARROT AND
WHITE TURNIP SOUP
....

Serve this soup as the first course to an elegant dinner. It complements roast chicken and duck beautifully.

*1 pound carrots, peeled and
   sliced*
*½ pound white turnips, peeled
   and sliced*
1 yellow onion, minced
3 tablespoons unsalted butter

3 tablespoons flour
6 cups chicken stock or *broth*
Salt
White pepper
1 cup light cream or *milk*
Snipped fresh chives for garnish

In a large saucepan over moderately low heat, melt the butter. Cook the carrots, turnips, and onion in the butter, covered, stirring occasionally, for 8 minutes. Add the flour and cook the mixture, stirring, for 2 minutes. Add the stock and salt and pepper to taste. Simmer, covered, stirring occasionally, for 45 minutes, or until the carrots are very tender.

Puree the soup in batches in a food processor or blender, and return to the saucepan. Stir in the cream and simmer, stirring, until it is heated through. Serve garnished with the chives. Makes about 9 cups, serving 6.

APPETIZERS
AND SNACKS

CARROT, MUSHROOM, AND WALNUT PÂTÉ

••

Serve this pâté, chilled, with Cucumber Dill Sauce (p. 19) and toasted Pita Chips (p. 22).

1 cup minced onion
4 large cloves garlic, minced
3 tablespoons unsalted butter, melted
½ pound fresh shiitake or white mushrooms, minced
½ teaspoon dried thyme, crumbled
4 cups grated carrots

4 large eggs, beaten lightly
1 cup ground walnuts, toasted lightly
½ cup grated Gruyère or Swiss cheese
½ cup grated Parmesan
½ cup minced fresh parsley
Salt
Pepper

Preheat the oven to 350° F.

In a skillet over moderate heat, cook the onion and garlic in the butter, stirring occasionally, for 5 minutes. Add the mushrooms and cook, stirring occasionally, for an additional 7 minutes, or until the liquid has evaporated.

Puree the mixture in a food processor or blender until well combined and transfer it to a bowl. Add the carrots, eggs, walnuts, cheeses, parsley, and salt and pepper to taste. Transfer the mixture to a buttered 9″ × 5″ × 2¾″ loaf pan and cover with a double layer of buttered foil. Set the loaf pan in a baking pan, add enough hot water to reach halfway up the sides of the loaf pan, and bake the pâté for 1 to 1½ hours, or until a skewer comes out clean. Transfer the loaf pan to a rack, let it cool to room temperature, and chill overnight.

Invert the pâté onto a platter and serve. Serves 6.

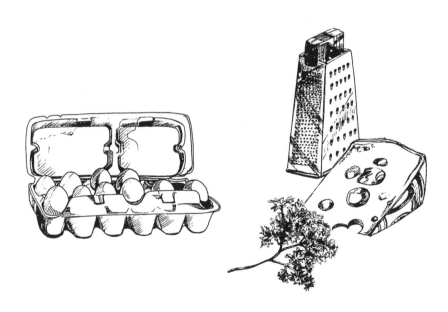

THE BIG CARROT BOOK

CUCUMBER DILL SAUCE

You can serve this sauce with the Carrot, Mushroom, and Walnut Pâté (p. 17), but try it with Carrot, Potato, and Scallion Fritters (p. 20) as well.

1 cucumber (about ½ pound), peeled, seeded, and finely grated
4 tablespoons lemon juice
½ teaspoon salt
⅓ cup minced scallions

1 cup sour cream or *drained plain yogurt (p. 27)*
2 tablespoons snipped fresh dill
1 clove garlic, minced
Salt
Pepper

In a colander, toss the cucumber with 1 tablespoon of the lemon juice and the salt and let it drain for 20 minutes. Squeeze dry.

In a bowl, combine the cucumber with the remaining lemon juice, scallions, sour cream, dill, and garlic. Chill the sauce, covered, for at least 1 hour. Add salt and pepper to taste just before serving. Makes about 1½ cups.

CARROT, POTATO, AND
SCALLION FRITTERS

•••••••••••••••••••••••••••

For maximum flavor serve these crisp and piping hot.

⅓ cup all-purpose flour
¼ teaspoon baking powder
Salt
2 large eggs
½ cup milk

1 cup grated carrots
½ cup grated potatoes
3 whole scallions, finely minced
Vegetable oil

Into a bowl, sift together the flour, baking powder, and salt. Whisk in the eggs and milk and continue to whisk until smooth. Stir in the carrots, potatoes, and scallions.

In a deep-fat fryer or heavy saucepan, heat the oil to 375° F. Drop heaping tablespoons of the mixture into the oil in batches and fry for 1 to 2 minutes on each side, turning the fritters until they are golden brown. With a slotted spoon, transfer the fritters to paper towels to drain. Serve with Cucumber Dill Sauce (p. 19). Makes about 12 fritters.

THE BIG CARROT BOOK

HERBED CARROT, CHEESE, AND LEMON DIP

Serve this dip with crudités—it's a cinch to put together quickly.

8 ounces cream cheese, softened
1 cup sour cream or *drained*
  plain yogurt (p. 27)
1 cup grated carrots
2 tablespoons lemon juice
1 teaspoon grated lemon peel

2 tablespoons each minced fresh
  parsley and chives or *scallion*
  tops
Salt
Pepper

In a bowl, combine the cream cheese and sour cream, stirring the mixture until smooth. Fold in the carrots, lemon juice, lemon peel, herbs, and salt and pepper. Makes about 2½ cups.

PITA CHIPS

Far more delicious than tortilla chips, these flavorful toasts are easy to prepare in advance and reheat beautifully.

6 tablespoons unsalted butter,
  softened
2 tablespoons minced fresh
  parsley
1 garlic clove, minced

Salt
Pepper
6 pita breads, halved
  horizontally, each half cut
  into two pieces

Preheat oven to 450° F.

In a bowl, combine the butter, parsley, garlic, and salt and pepper to taste. Spread the inside of each pita bread with some of the seasoned butter and arrange on a baking sheet in one layer. Toast for 5 minutes, or until golden brown. Makes 24 chips.

CARROT AND DILLED
CREAM CHEESE PINWHEELS

....

These lovely little hors d'oeuvres are best prepared several hours ahead of time.

4 ounces cream cheese, softened
1 tablespoon snipped fresh dill
1 tablespoon snipped fresh
    chives or scallion tops
1 tablespoon minced parsley
1 tablespoon finely minced
    scallions

1 teaspoon grated lemon peel
Salt
Pepper
4 carrots, peeled

In a bowl, combine the cream cheese, dill, chives, parsley, scallions, lemon peel, and salt and pepper to taste.

With a vegetable peeler, cut ½″–¾″ wide strips along the length of each carrot, spread some of the cheese mixture on each strip and roll up to make pinwheels. Chill, covered, for at least 1 hour or overnight. Makes about 36 pinwheels.

CARROT, LEEK, AND CELERY TART

....

This tart is wonderful served hot or at room temperature. It makes a perfect light lunch when served with a tossed salad.

3 carrots, peeled and cut into 1-inch julienne strips
2 large leeks (white part only), cut into 1-inch julienne strips
1 large celery rib, cut into 1-inch julienne strips
3 cloves garlic, minced
3 tablespoons butter, melted
Salt
Freshly ground pepper
3 large eggs
½ cup milk, light cream or heavy cream
½ cup freshly grated Parmesan
3 tablespoons minced fresh parsley
1 9-inch prebaked pie shell

Preheat oven to 375° F.

In a large saucepan over moderately low heat, cook the carrots, leeks, celery, garlic, and salt and pepper in the butter. Cover with a round of wax paper and the lid, and cook, stirring occasionally, for 10 minutes.

In a bowl, whisk together the eggs, milk, Parmesan, parsley, and salt and pepper to taste. Spoon vegetable mixture evenly into pie shell, and top with egg mixture. Bake tart on a baking sheet for 30 to 35 minutes, or until golden brown and set. Let cool until warm, and cut into wedges. Serves 6 as an appetizer, 4 as an entrée.

CARROT BLINI

Serve these as appetizers or for a light lunch.

1 ½ cups all-purpose flour
2 teaspoons baking powder
Salt
1 ½ cups milk
1 extra-large egg

6 tablespoons unsalted butter,
  melted
1 recipe Carrot Puree (p. 28)
Vegetable oil
Chive Cream (p. 26)

Preheat oven to 200° F.

Into a bowl, sift the flour, baking powder, and salt. In another bowl, whisk together the milk, egg, and butter. Add the flour mixture and Carrot Puree to the milk mixture, stirring just to combine.

Brush a heated griddle or large nonstick skillet with oil. Spoon the batter in ¼ cups onto the griddle, smoothing into rounds, and cook for 1 to 2 minutes on each side, or until golden brown. Transfer the blini to a buttered baking sheet and keep them warm in the oven. Serve the blini with Chive Cream (p. 26). Serves 6 as a first course or 4 as an entrée.

CHIVE CREAM

....

An excellent accompaniment for Carrot Blini (p. 25) or as an addition to the hors d'oeuvres tray.

8 ounces cream cheese, softened
⅔ cup sour cream
Salt
Cayenne pepper

Lemon juice to taste
¼ cup snipped fresh chives or
scallion tops

In a bowl, whisk together the cream cheese, sour cream, salt, cayenne, and lemon juice until smooth. Stir in the chives. Makes about 2 cups.

DILLED YOGURT CREAM

This delicious cream may be used as a dip for vegetables and chips, or as a garnish for soups.

1 cup low-fat plain yogurt   *Salt*
¼ cup sour cream   *Pepper*
3 tablespoons snipped fresh dill

In a sieve lined with a double thickness of rinsed and squeezed cheesecloth, let the yogurt drain for 20 minutes. Transfer the yogurt to a bowl and add the remaining ingredients. Makes about 1 cup.

CARROT PUREE

· ·

This versatile puree forms the base for many recipes in this book. It is equally good on its own as a side dish, and makes a wonderful accompaniment to roast poultry and meat.

1 pound carrots, peeled and sliced

In a steamer or rack set over boiling water, steam the carrots, covered, for 10 minutes, or until tender. Transfer the carrots to a food processor or blender and puree them until smooth. Makes about 1⅓ cups.

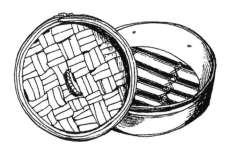

PICKLED CARROT STICKS

These make a wonderful and unusual addition to your holiday relish tray.

1 pound carrots, peeled and cut into 3″ × ½″ batons
¾ cup white wine vinegar
¼ cup balsamic vinegar
1 cup water

2 tablespoons sugar
1 tablespoon salt
2 teaspoons mustard seeds
1 teaspoon celery seeds
2 red pepper pods

In a large saucepan of boiling salted water, blanch the carrots for 1 minute. Drain and refresh them under ice-cold water. Divide the carrots, standing them upright, between two 1-pint preserving jars.

In a saucepan, combine the vinegars, water, sugar, salt, mustard seeds, celery seeds, and red pepper pods, bring the mixture to a boil, and boil 1 minute. Divide the vinegar mixture between the jars, filling each jar to within ¼ inch of the top. Make sure that 1 pepper pod is in each. Refrigerate the sealed jars for at least 1 day or for up to 1 week. Makes 2 pints.

SALADS

GRATED CARROT SALAD WITH TOASTED CUMIN SEEDS AND CILANTRO

A light and refreshing salad.

FOR THE SALAD:
- 1 pound carrots, peeled and grated
- ½ cup minced shallots or scallions
- 2 tablespoons minced fresh cilantro
- 1 tablespoon cumin seeds, toasted

FOR THE DRESSING:
- 2 tablespoons lemon juice
- 2 tablespoons olive oil
- Salt
- Pepper

In a bowl combine the carrots, shallots, cilantro and cumin seeds. Add the lemon juice, olive oil, and salt and pepper to taste, tossing to combine. Serves 4.

CARROT, RED CABBAGE, AND
ROQUEFORT SLAW WITH WALNUTS

· ·

This unusual combination is enhanced by the flavor of Roquefort cheese. Serve with toasted croutons.

FOR THE SALAD:

1 pound red cabbage, cored and
    thinly sliced
1 Golden Delicious apple,
    peeled, cored, and thinly sliced
4 carrots, peeled and grated
1 onion, finely minced
¼ pound Roquefort or blue
    cheese, crumbled
⅓ cup coarsely chopped toasted
    walnuts

FOR THE DRESSING:

¼ cup cider vinegar or white
    wine vinegar
¼ cup vegetable oil
1 tablespoon Dijon mustard
1 tablespoon sugar
Salt
Pepper

MAKE THE SALAD: In a large bowl, combine the cabbage, apple, carrots, onion, Roquefort, and walnuts.

MAKE THE DRESSING: In a small bowl, whisk together the vinegar, oil, mustard, sugar, and salt and pepper. Add the dressing to the salad and toss to combine. Serves 6.

CARROT, WHITE RADISH, AND SPINACH SALAD

In France this is known as a *salade composée*. Unlike most salads, the ingredients are not tossed together, but grouped separately on a serving plate; the dressing is served on the side. It is a wonderful salad for an elegant lunch and makes a beautiful presentation on a buffet table.

FOR THE SALAD:
4 cups grated carrots
2 cups grated white radishes
2 cups thinly sliced spinach
  leaves

FOR THE DRESSING:
3 tablespoons lemon juice
3 tablespoons white wine vinegar
2 tablespoons Dijon mustard
Salt
Pepper
½ to ⅔ cup olive or *vegetable oil*

MAKE THE SALAD: On a serving plate, arrange in alternate rows the carrots, radishes, and spinach.

MAKE THE DRESSING: In a bowl, whisk together the lemon juice, vinegar, mustard, and salt and pepper. Add the oil in a stream, whisking until the dressing is combined well. Serves 6.

JULIENNED CARROT, SNOWPEA, AND RED PEPPER SALAD WITH SHRIMP AND TOASTED SESAME SEEDS

A crisp and refreshing salad that is particularly good for lunch during the warm-weather months.

FOR THE SALAD:

½ pound carrots, peeled and cut into 2-inch julienned strips

1 large red bell pepper, cut lengthwise into ¼-inch wide strips

1 pound large shrimp, shelled and deveined

¼ pound snowpeas, cut lengthwise into ¼-inch wide strips

8-ounce can straw mushrooms, drained

½ cup thinly sliced scallions

FOR THE DRESSING:

2 tablespoons rice vinegar or white wine vinegar

1 tablespoon lemon juice

2 teaspoons minced fresh gingerroot

2 teaspoons Dijon mustard

1 clove garlic, finely minced

Salt

Pepper

3 tablespoons vegetable oil

2 tablespoons Oriental sesame oil

1 tablespoon toasted sesame seeds for garnish

MAKE THE SALAD: In a large saucepan of boiling salted water, simmer the carrots for 1 minute. Add the bell pepper and shrimp and simmer for 1 minute more. Add the snowpeas and straw mushrooms and simmer for 30 seconds to 1 minute, or until the shrimp are opaque but still springy to the touch. Drain, refresh under ice-cold water and pat dry. In a salad bowl, combine the carrot mixture and scallions.

MAKE THE DRESSING: In a bowl, whisk together the rice vinegar, lemon juice, ginger, mustard, garlic, and salt and pepper. Add the oils in a stream, whisking until the mixture is combined well. Add the dressing to the salad and toss to combine. Sprinkle with the sesame seeds. Serves 4 as an entrée, 6 as an appetizer.

ORIENTAL CARROT, CHICKEN, AND NOODLE SALAD WITH PEANUT SAUCE

....

There are countless variations to this salad. Shellfish, such as shrimp or scallops, may be substituted for the chicken. In addition to the carrot and cucumber, broccoli, baby corn, and red bell peppers may also be included.

FOR THE SALAD:

½ pound thin Chinese egg noodles or spaghettini, cooked al dente, drained and refreshed
1 tablespoon Oriental sesame oil
2 cups shredded cooked chicken
2 cups thinly sliced carrots
1 cup cucumber, peeled, seeded, and diced
½ cup minced scallions
2 tablespoons minced fresh cilantro

FOR THE PEANUT SAUCE:

⅓ cup smooth peanut butter
⅓ cup canned chicken broth or water
2 tablespoons soy sauce
2 tablespoons Oriental sesame oil
1 tablespoon minced garlic
1 tablespoon minced fresh gingerroot
1 tablespoon honey
1 tablespoon rice vinegar or cider vinegar
¼ teaspoon red pepper flakes
Salt
Pepper
¼ cup coarsely chopped dry-roasted peanuts

MAKE THE SALAD: In a large bowl, toss the noodles with the sesame oil. Add the chicken, carrots, cucumber, scallions, and cilantro and stir gently to combine.

MAKE THE SAUCE: In a blender or food processor, combine the sauce ingredients and blend until well combined. Add the dressing to the salad and toss thoroughly. Sprinkle with the peanuts. Serves 6.

INDIAN-STYLE CARROT, CUCUMBER, AND YOGURT SALAD

··

This cooling, relish-type salad complements rice and hearty stews especially well. It's also wonderful as an accompaniment to sandwiches or fried chicken.

1 ½ cups drained plain yogurt
  (p. 27)
½ cup sour cream
1 tablespoons lemon juice
1 teaspoon toasted cumin seeds,
  ground
Salt

Cayenne pepper
2 cups grated carrots
1 cup seeded and grated cucum-
  ber, squeezed dry
1 cup diced red bell pepper
2 tablespoons minced fresh mint
  or cilantro

In a bowl, whisk together the yogurt, sour cream, lemon juice, and cumin seeds. Add salt and cayenne pepper to taste. Mix in the carrots, cucumber, bell pepper, and mint, stirring gently until the mixture is combined. Serves 4.

CARROT AND FUSILLI SALAD PRIMAVERA

As its name implies, this salad is best when made with spring vegetables. Vary the vegetables according to taste and, if desired, add cooked seafood or chicken to make a sumptuous meal.

FOR THE SALAD:

1 pound fusilli or other similar pasta

1 pound carrots, trimmed, peeled and sliced

½ pound asparagus, trimmed and cut into 1-inch pieces

2 zucchini, trimmed and cut into ½-inch cubes

1 cup fresh or thawed frozen peas

1 red bell pepper, diced

½ cup minced scallions

FOR THE DRESSING:

1 cup loosely packed basil leaves

4 garlic cloves, chopped

4 tablespoons white wine vinegar

2 tablespoons Dijon mustard

Salt

Pepper

¼ cup olive oil

¼ cup vegetable oil

⅓ cup toasted pine nuts

½ cup freshly grated Parmesan

MAKE THE SALAD: In a large saucepan of boiling salted water, cook the pasta for 5 minutes, or until it is barely al dente. Add the carrots, and cook for 3 minutes more. Add the asparagus, zucchini, and peas and cook, stirring, for 3 minutes more. Drain and refresh under ice-cold water. Pat dry. Transfer the mixture to a large bowl and add the pepper and scallions.

MAKE THE DRESSING: In a blender or processor, combine the basil, garlic, vinegar, mustard, and salt and pepper and blend until it is mixed well. With the motor running, add the oils in a stream and blend until the dressing is combined well. Drizzle the dressing over the pasta and toss gently to combine. Garnish with the pine nuts and serve with the Parmesan. Serves 6–8.

BLACK-EYED PEA AND RICE SALAD
WITH CARROTS AND FRESH THYME

This recipe is a variation on the classic New Year's Day dish Hoppin' John. Here, it is served at room temperature with the addition of a few vegetables and a vinaigrette dressing.

3 cups cooked black-eyed peas
   or 3 cups canned black-eyed
   peas, well drained
3 cups cooked rice
3 cups cooked sliced carrots
1 cup minced red onion
1 cup diced bell pepper
½ cup diced celery

1 tablespoon minced fresh thyme
   or 1 teaspoon dried, crumbled
⅓ cup cider vinegar
2 tablespoons sugar
Salt
Pepper
⅓ cup vegetable oil
2 tablespoons minced fresh
   parsley

In a large bowl, combine the peas, rice, carrots, onion, bell pepper, celery, and thyme. In a small bowl, whisk together the vinegar, sugar, and salt and pepper to taste. Add the oil in a stream, whisking until the dressing is well combined. Pour the dressing over the salad and toss gently to combine. Sprinkle with the parsley. Serves 6.

ENTRÉES

BRAISED BRISKET WITH CARROTS AND PRUNES

••

This is a one-pot meal, ideal for Sunday dinner.

2 tablespoons vegetable oil
3-pound brisket of beef
Salt
Pepper
2 tablespoons butter
2 large onions, thinly sliced
4 cloves garlic, minced
3 tablespoons flour
3 cups beef broth
1 tablespoon tomato paste

1 bay leaf
1 teaspoon dried savory,
    crumbled
1 stick cinnamon, cracked
6 cloves
1 tablespoon grated orange peel
2 pounds carrots, quartered
½ pound pitted prunes
1 tablespoon lemon juice

Preheat the oven to 350° F.

In a casserole set over moderately high heat, heat the oil. When hot, season the brisket with salt and pepper, add to the casserole, and brown on all sides.

Transfer the meat to a platter. Pour off the fat from the pan and add the butter. Add the onion and garlic and cook the vegetables over moderate heat, stirring occasionally, for 5 minutes. Add the flour and cook the mixture for 2 minutes, stirring constantly. Add the broth, tomato paste, bay leaf, savory, cinnamon, cloves, and orange peel. Return the brisket to the casserole along with any accumulated juices and bring the liquid to a simmer. Braise the brisket, covered, in the oven for 1½ hours. Add the carrots and prunes and braise for 1 hour more, or until the brisket is tender. Stir in the lemon juice and correct the seasoning. Serves 6.

SAUTÉED CHICKEN BREASTS IN FENNEL-SCENTED CARROT SAUCE

••

Like ginger, fennel has an affinity for carrots. Here they are combined to create an elegant sauce for chicken.

FOR THE SAUCE:
2 tablespoons butter
½ pound carrots, peeled and
    chopped
1 small McIntosh apple, peeled,
    cored, and chopped
1 cup minced onion
½ cup minced fennel (bulb only)
2 large cloves garlic, minced
1 teaspoon fennel seeds, crushed
½ teaspoon dried rosemary,
    crumbled
1 bay leaf
Salt

Pepper
1 cup chicken broth

FOR THE CHICKEN:
2 boned chicken breasts, halved
Salt
Pepper
½ teaspoon dried rosemary,
    crumbled
2 tablespoons olive oil
½ cup heavy or light cream
Lemon juice to taste
2 tablespoons minced fresh
    parsley

MAKE THE SAUCE: Melt the butter in a saucepan, and cook the carrots, apple, onion, fennel, garlic, fennel seeds, rosemary, bay leaf, and salt and pepper over moderately low heat, covered with a buttered round of wax paper and the lid, stirring occasionally, for 10 minutes. Add the broth to the mixture and simmer, covered, for 15 minutes, or until the vegetables are soft. Discard bay leaf. In a food processor or blender, puree the carrot mixture until smooth and return it to the pan.

MAKE THE CHICKEN: Season the chicken breasts with the salt, pepper, and rosemary. In a skillet, heat the oil over moderately high heat. When hot, add the chicken and brown for 2 minutes on each side. Reduce the heat to moderate and cook the chicken, covered, for 8 to 10 minutes more, or until it is cooked through. Transfer the chicken to a platter. Pour off the fat from the skillet and deglaze the pan with the carrot puree, scraping up the brown bits clinging to the bottom. Stir in the cream, lemon juice, and salt and pepper to taste, bring to a simmer and strain the sauce over the chicken. Sprinkle with the parsley. Serves 4.

THE BIG CARROT BOOK

BABY CARROTS AND SALMON *EN PAPILLOTE*

Cooking "*en papillote*" is a method by which food is sealed in parchment paper or foil and baked in the oven. The food cooks in its own juices, resulting in deliciously concentrated flavors.

8 baby carrots, peeled and trimmed
16 pearl onions, peeled and trimmed
16 asparagus tips
2 tablespoons extra-virgin olive oil
2 teaspoons grated lemon peel
Salt
Pepper
1½ pounds center-cut salmon fillet, cut crosswise into 4 pieces
2 tablespoons snipped fresh dill

In a large saucepan of boiling salted water, cook the carrots and onions for 4 minutes. Add the asparagus tips and cook the vegetables for 2 minutes more, or until the carrots and onions are just tender. Refresh the vegetables under ice-cold water, and pat dry. In a bowl, combine the vegetables, oil, lemon peel, and salt and pepper to taste.

Preheat oven to 425° F.

Cut out 4 heart shapes, each about 14 inches long through the center, from parchment paper or foil. Grease 1 side of each heart and put a salmon fillet in the center. Arrange the vegetables decoratively around the salmon and season the fish with salt and pepper. Beginning with the top edge of each heart, fold and crimp the sides of the hearts together to seal the packets. Bake the packets on a baking sheet in the oven for 15 minutes.

Transfer the packets to serving plates and cut a cross in the top of each. Fold back the edges and sprinkle with the dill or serve with Dilled Mustard Sauce (p. 53). Serves 4.

DILLED MUSTARD SAUCE

This is a very versatile sauce, particularly good with fish and vegetables.

½ cup minced shallots
½ cup dry white wine
1 cup chicken broth
1 cup heavy cream

4 tablespoons Dijon mustard, or
  to taste
2 tablespoons fresh dill, chives,
  or parsley

In a small saucepan, combine the shallots and wine and reduce over medium high heat to 2 tablespoons. Add the broth and reduce the mixture by half. Add the cream and boil until the sauce is slightly thickened. Before serving, whisk in the mustard and dill. Makes about 1 cup.

PARSLEYED CARROT ROULADE

This is an unusual brunch dish that will delight your guests. Serve the roulade with the Cucumber Dill Sauce (p. 19) *or* Chive Cream (p. 26).

FOR THE BATTER:
3 tablespoons unsalted butter
⅓ cup all-purpose flour
1¼ cups milk, heated
1 tablespoon Dijon mustard
Salt
Cayenne pepper
4 large eggs, separated
½ cup grated Parmesan

FOR THE FILLING:
1 recipe Carrot Puree (p. 28)
½ cup grated Fontina cheese
2 tablespoons grated Parmesan
2 tablespoons minced fresh
    parsley
1 tablespoon melted butter
1 tablespoon grated Parmesan

Preheat oven to 350° F.

MAKE THE BATTER: In a saucepan over moderately low heat, melt the butter, add the flour, and cook the mixture for 2 minutes, whisking continuously. Add the milk, bring to a boil, and simmer for 5 minutes, whisking occasionally, or until thickened. Stir in the mustard, salt, and cayenne. Transfer the mixture to a bowl, whisk in the egg yolks, one at a time, along with the Parmesan. In a bowl, beat the whites with an electric mixer until they form soft peaks. Stir ¼ of the whites into the yolk mixture and then fold in the remaining whites.

Thoroughly butter a 10½″ × 15½″ jelly-roll pan, line it with parchment or wax paper and butter and flour the paper. Spread the batter evenly in the pan and bake the roulade for 20 to 25 minutes, or until golden and set. Cover the roulade with a sheet of buttered parchment or wax paper, buttered side down. Place a baking sheet over it and invert the roulade onto the baking sheet. Remove the pan and wax paper and trim the edges.

MAKE THE FILLING: In a bowl, combine the filling ingredients. Spread this mixture over the warm roulade in an even layer, leaving a 1-inch border. Roll the roulade jelly-roll fashion, beginning with a long side, and trim the ends diagonally. Transfer the roulade, seam side down, to a baking sheet. Brush it with the melted butter and sprinkle with the Parmesan. Bake for 10 minutes, or until heated through. Serve with the Cucumber Dill Sauce or Chive Cream. Serves 4.

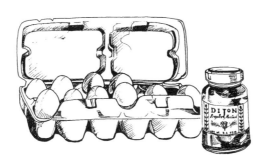

CURRIED CARROT AND BARLEY PILAF

Serve this on a cold winter night.

2 tablespoons olive oil
2 cups minced onion
4 cloves garlic, minced
1 tablespoon minced gingerroot
1 tablespoon curry powder, or to
   taste
1 cup medium pearl barley
Salt
Pepper
1 teaspoon ground cumin
½ teaspoon ground cinnamon
1 bay leaf

2 ½ cups chicken broth
14 ½-ounce can tomatoes, puréed
   with the liquid
6 carrots, peeled and cut diagonally into thick slices
1 large zucchini, cut into 1-inch
   cubes
1 16-ounce can chickpeas,
   drained and rinsed
2 tablespoons minced fresh
   cilantro

Heat the oil in a large saucepan over moderate heat. When it is hot, add the onion and cook, stirring occasionally, for 5 minutes. Add the garlic, ginger, and curry powder. Cook the mixture, stirring, for 1 minute more. Add the barley, salt, pepper, cumin, cinnamon, and bay leaf. Cook and stir 1 minute more, then add the broth and tomatoes. Bring to a boil and simmer the mixture, covered, for 30 minutes. Add the carrots and cover; cook for 15 minutes. Add the zucchini and chickpeas; cover, and cook 5 minutes more. Sprinkle with the cilantro. Serves 4.

CARROT AND VEGETABLE COUSCOUS

To make this a true vegetarian dish, substitute vegetable broth *or* water for chicken broth.

2 tablespoons olive oil
4 cups sliced onions
6 carrots, peeled and thickly
    sliced
4 small white turnips, cut into
    1-inch pieces
4 cloves garlic, minced
4 cups chicken broth
14½-ounce can tomatoes, puréed
    with the liquid
1 teaspoon each dried thyme and
    basil
½ teaspoon each ground ginger
    and cinnamon

Salt
Pepper
1 bay leaf
1 zucchini, trimmed and cut into
    1-inch cubes
1 yellow squash, trimmed and
    cut into 1-inch cubes
2 cups canned chickpeas, rinsed
    and drained
⅓ cup each diced dried apricots
    and raisins
1 tablespoon butter
1 cup couscous

In a casserole set over moderate heat, heat the oil. When it is hot, add the onions and cook until lightly golden, stirring occasionally. Add the carrots, turnips, and garlic and cook, stirring, for 2 minutes. Add the broth, tomatoes, thyme, basil, ginger, cinnamon, salt, pepper, and bay leaf. Bring the liquid to a boil and simmer the vegetables, covered, for 8–10 minutes. Add the zucchini, squash, and chickpeas and simmer, covered, until the vegetables are just tender, about 6 minutes. Discard bay leaf. Stir in the apricots and raisins.

In a small saucepan, combine 1½ cups of the vegetable cooking liquid with the butter, bring to a boil and add the couscous. Let stand 10 minutes, or until the liquid is absorbed. Serve the vegetables over the couscous. Serves 4 to 6.

CARROT, TOFU, AND RICE CASSEROLE WITH TOASTED ALMONDS

••••••••••••••••••••••••••••••••••••

This is a perfect one-pot meal. Serve it with a crisp green salad.

3 tablespoons olive oil
2 cups minced onions
2 cups sliced carrots
1 cup diced red bell pepper
Salt
Pepper
1 cup drained and chopped
   canned tomatoes
1 tablespoon minced garlic
½ teaspoon ground turmeric
½ teaspoon each dried rosemary
   and basil, crumbled

3 ½ cups chicken broth
1 bay leaf
2 cups long-grain white rice
1 pound firm tofu, drained and
   cut into 1-inch cubes
½ cup sliced almonds, blanched
   and toasted
2 tablespoons minced
   fresh parsley

Preheat the oven to 350° F.

Heat the oil in a casserole set over moderate heat. When hot, add the onions, carrots, pepper, salt, and bell peppers. Cover and cook the vegetables for 5 minutes, stirring occasionally. Add the tomatoes, garlic, turmeric, rosemary, and basil and cook, stirring occasionally, until thick. Stir in the broth and bay leaf. Bring to a boil, stir in the rice and tofu. Cover and bake the casserole for 25 to 30 minutes, or until the rice is tender. Let stand 5 minutes and sprinkle with the almonds and parsley. Serves 4–6.

SIDE DISHES

ORANGE-GINGERED CARROTS

A family favorite. Carrots prepared this way are a delicious accompaniment to broiled and roasted poultry and meats.

*1 pound carrots, peeled and cut
    into 1-inch pieces
½ cup fresh orange juice
3 tablespoons honey*

*2 tablespoons unsalted butter
1 ½ teaspoons minced fresh gin-
    gerroot, or ¼ teaspoon ground
1 teaspoon grated orange peel*

In a saucepan, combine the carrots, orange juice, honey, butter, gingerroot, and orange peel. Salt and pepper to taste, and add enough water to just cover. Bring the liquid to a boil, and simmer, covered, for 6 to 8 minutes, or until the carrots are just tender. Increase the heat to high and cook, uncovered, until the liquid has reduced to ¼ cup. Cook the carrots, shaking the pan, until the liquid is almost completely reduced and the carrots are glazed. Serves 4.

CARROTS BAKED IN MUSTARD CREAM SAUCE

Since this dish can be completely prepared ahead of time, it is perfect dinner-party fare.

1 ½ pounds carrots, peeled and
* grated*
1 cup light cream
1 cup milk
2 teaspoons cornstarch
2 tablespoons Dijon mustard
1 teaspoon dried rosemary,
* crumbled*

⅓ cup freshly grated Parmesan
⅓ cup dried breadcrumbs
2 tablespoons minced fresh pars-
* ley*
1 tablespoon butter, cut into bits

Preheat the oven to 425° F.

In a large saucepan of boiling salted water, cook the carrots for 1 minute, drain and refresh them under ice-cold water. Pat dry. Transfer the carrots to a shallow buttered baking dish.

In a bowl, whisk together the cream, milk, cornstarch, mustard, and rosemary. Add salt and pepper to taste, and pour the mixture over the carrots. (Dish may be prepared up to 6 hours in advance to this point and kept covered and chilled.) In a bowl, combine the Parmesan, breadcrumbs, and parsley. Sprinkle the Parmesan mixture over the top of the dish, dot with butter, and bake in the oven for 25 to 30 minutes or until golden brown. Serves 6.

GLAZED CARROTS AND TURNIPS

This combination of carrots and turnips makes a delicious side dish with poultry and game.

1 cup canned chicken broth
2 tablespoons unsalted butter
1 tablespoon sugar
Salt
Pepper

1 ½ pounds carrots, peeled and sliced
1 ½ pounds turnips, sliced
2 tablespoons minced fresh parsley

In a saucepan, combine the broth, butter, sugar, salt, pepper, and carrots, bring the liquid to a boil and simmer the carrots for 2 minutes. Add the turnips, and simmer, covered, for 5 minutes longer, or until the vegetables are tender. Transfer the vegetables to a serving dish, and reduce the cooking liquid over moderately high heat to ¼ cup. Pour the sauce over the vegetables and sprinkle with the parsley. Serves 6.

CARROT, LEEK, AND POTATO GRATIN

Accompany this gratin with a salad and some crusty bread for a warming lunch or light supper.

1 pound carrots, peeled and
  sliced
2 medium-large Idaho potatoes,
  peeled and sliced
2 large leeks (white and pale
  green parts), well washed and
  chopped
3 tablespoons butter

2 tablespoons flour
2 cups milk
⅓ cup grated Parmesan
⅓ cup grated Gruyère
1 tablespoon Dijon mustard
Freshly grated nutmeg to taste
Salt
Pepper

Preheat oven to 350° F.

In a saucepan, cover the carrots and potatoes with water, bring to a boil and simmer for 2 minutes. Drain. Transfer the carrots and potatoes to a buttered gratin dish.

In a saucepan over moderate heat, cook the leeks in 2 tablespoons of the butter, stirring, until softened. Add the flour, and cook the mixture over low heat, stirring, for 3 minutes. Add the milk, bring the liquid to a boil and simmer, stirring occasionally, for 5 minutes. Stir in 4 tablespoons each of the Parmesan and Gruyère, and add the mustard, nutmeg, and salt and pepper to taste.

Spoon the leek mixture over the carrots and potatoes, sprinkle the top with the remaining cheeses, and dot with the remaining butter. Bake for 40 minutes, or until potatoes and carrots are tender. Serves 6.

CARROT TIMBALES

Certainly one of the most elegant ways to serve carrots, this recipe may be prepared in advance and reheated before serving.

1 pound carrots, peeled and finely chopped
½ cup finely chopped shallots
1 teaspoon sugar
Salt
Pepper
3 tablespoons butter

¾ cup chicken broth
1 bay leaf
2 large eggs, beaten lightly
3 tablespoons snipped fresh dill
3 tablespoons grated Parmesan
Dilled Mustard Sauce (p. 53) as an accompaniment (optional)

Preheat oven to 350° F.

In a saucepan set over moderate heat, cook the carrots, shallots, sugar, and salt and pepper in the butter, stirring occasionally, for 5 minutes. Add the broth and bay leaf, and simmer the mixture, covered, for 10 minutes. Increase the heat to moderately high and simmer the mixture, uncovered, until the liquid is evaporated. Let cool and remove the bay leaf. In a bowl, whisk together the eggs, dill, and Parmesan. Add the carrot mixture and stir to combine.

Divide the mixture among four ½-cup buttered ramekins and cover with foil. Set the ramekins in a baking pan, add enough hot water to the pan to reach halfway up the sides of the ramekins, and bake in the oven for 30 minutes, or until a knife inserted in the centers comes out clean. Remove the foil, run a thin knife around the inside edge of ramekins and invert the timbales onto plates. Serve with the Dilled Mustard Sauce, if desired. Serves 4.

SAUTÉED CARROTS, PEARL ONIONS, AND BRUSSELS SPROUTS IN LEMON BUTTER

••

This is a lovely addition to the holiday table.

1 pound carrots, peeled and cut
    diagonally into 1-inch thick
    pieces
1 pound pearl onions, peeled
Salt
Pepper

¾ pound brussels sprouts,
    trimmed
3 tablespoons butter
½ teaspoon grated lemon peel
1 tablespoon lemon juice

In a large saucepan, combine the carrots, onions, and salt and pepper to taste with enough water to cover the vegetables by 2 inches. Bring to a boil and simmer for 2 minutes. Add the brussels sprouts and simmer the vegetables for 8 to 10 minutes more, or until they are tender. Drain.

In the saucepan, melt the butter over moderate heat and add the lemon peel. Return the vegetables to the pan, and toss to coat with the butter. Cook until heated through. Before serving, season with salt, pepper, and lemon juice. Serves 6.

THE BIG CARROT BOOK

SAUTÉED CARROTS WITH GARLIC, BLACK OLIVES, AND PARSLEY

····································

A very quick, easy recipe redolent with the flavors of southern France.

3 tablespoons olive oil
*1 pound carrots, peeled and
    sliced ½-inch thick*
6 cloves garlic, peeled and halved
Salt

Pepper
*½ cup chopped pitted black
    olives, such as Calamata or
    Niçoise*
2 tablespoons minced parsley

In a large skillet, heat the oil. When hot, add the carrots, garlic, salt and pepper and cook the mixture, stirring, for 3 minutes. Reduce the heat to moderately low and simmer, covered, for 12 to 15 minutes more, or until the carrots are just tender. Add the olives and parsley and toss to combine. Serves 4.

CARROTS WITH BASIL OIL AND MINT

An unusual and delicately flavorful way to serve carrots—delicious hot or at room temperature.

1 pound carrots, peeled and sliced
2 tablespoons Basil Oil (p. 71)
1 tablespoon fresh lemon juice

2 tablespoons chopped fresh mint
Salt
Pepper

In a saucepan of boiling salted water, cook the carrots for 5 to 6 minutes, or until just tender. Drain and transfer to a bowl. Add the Basil Oil, lemon juice, mint, and salt and pepper to taste and toss the mixture until well combined. Serves 4.

BASIL OIL

. . . .

This oil may be used to flavor soups and vegetables, and as a dressing for salads.

2 bunches fresh basil, including   *2 cups extra-virgin olive oil*
*   stems, washed well*

In a large pot of boiling water, blanch the basil for 30 seconds. Drain and refresh under ice-cold water. Drain and gently squeeze dry.

In a food processor or blender, combine the basil with ¼ cup of the oil and process until a thick paste forms, scraping down the sides of the bowl. In a mason jar, combine the paste with the remaining olive oil and let it stand, tightly covered, for 2 days. Shake the jar each day.

Strain the mixture through a coffee filter and store in a tightly covered jar in the refrigerator. Makes about 1½ cups.

ROASTED CARROT AND APPLE PUREE

This puree is wonderful served with roast pork or duck.

8 carrots, peeled and cut into 1 ½-inch pieces
2 Granny Smith or McIntosh apples, peeled, cored, and quartered

⅓ cup chicken stock or broth
Freshly grated nutmeg to taste
Salt
Pepper

Preheat oven to 400° F.

In a buttered baking dish, roast the carrots for 25 minutes, stirring frequently. Add apples and continue to roast for 20 minutes more, or until tender. Transfer to a food processor and process until smooth.

Deglaze the roasting pan with the chicken stock, scraping up the brown bits clinging to the pan, reduce the liquid to ¼ cup, and add to the puree along with the nutmeg, salt, and pepper to taste. Process until combined well. Serves 4.

CREAMED BABY CARROTS WITH DILL

One of my favorite ways of preparing carrots. Chives or parsley may be used instead of dill.

1 pound baby carrots, trimmed and peeled
2 tablespoons butter
3 tablespoons minced shallots

1 cup heavy cream
2 tablespoons snipped fresh dill
Salt
Pepper

Place the carrots in a saucepan over moderately high heat with enough water to just cover. Add salt to taste. Bring to a boil, cover, and simmer for 10 minutes, or until tender. Drain.

Melt the butter in a skillet over moderate heat. Add the shallots, and cook, stirring, for 2 minutes. Add the cream and reduce over moderately high heat until slightly thickened. Stir in the dill. Return the carrots to the pan, toss to coat with the sauce, and season with salt and pepper to taste. Serves 4.

BREADS

CARROT AND TOASTED PECAN TEA BREAD

Decorated with colorful plastic wrap and tied with festive ribbons, this bread makes a perfect holiday or hostess gift.

2 ½ cups sifted all-purpose flour
1 ½ teaspoons baking powder
1 teaspoon baking soda
¾ teaspoon salt
1 ½ teaspoons cinnamon
½ teaspoon ground ginger
⅛ teaspoon ground cloves
½ cup granulated sugar

½ cup firmly packed light-brown
  sugar
2 cups coarsely grated carrots
1 cup chopped toasted pecans
2 large eggs, beaten lightly
1 ½ sticks unsalted butter, melted
½ cup orange juice
2 teaspoons grated orange peel

Preheat oven to 350° F.

Into a bowl, sift the flour, baking powder, baking soda, salt, cinnamon, ginger, and cloves. Add the sugars, carrots, and pecans. In another bowl, beat together the eggs, butter, orange juice, and orange peel. Stir the liquid ingredients into the flour mixture until combined. Pour into a well-buttered 9″ × 5″ × 3″ loaf pan and bake for 50–60 minutes, or until a cake tester inserted in the center comes out clean. If the top becomes too brown, cover loosely with foil. Let the bread cool in the pan on a rack for 5 minutes, then invert and cool completely. Makes 1 loaf.

SPICED CARROT AND APRICOT MUFFINS

Vary the seasonings according to taste. These lovely little muffins are wonderful for breakfast or as a snack.

½ cup finely chopped dried
   apricots
2 cups all-purpose flour
1 cup sugar
2 teaspoons baking soda
1½ teaspoons cinnamon
¼ teaspoon ground ginger
¼ teaspoon freshly grated
   nutmeg
½ teaspoon salt

2 cups grated carrots
1 large McIntosh apple, peeled,
   cored, and grated
1 cup chopped walnuts
½ cup unsweetened shredded
   coconut, toasted
3 large eggs
⅔ cup vegetable oil
1½ teaspoons vanilla
1½ teaspoons grated orange peel

Preheat oven to 350° F.

In a bowl, soak the apricots in hot water to cover for 30 minutes. Drain and pat dry. Into a large bowl, sift together the flour, sugar, baking soda, cinnamon, ginger, nutmeg, and salt. Add the apricots, carrots, apple, walnuts, and coconut. In a bowl, whisk together the eggs, oil, vanilla, and orange peel and stir the mixture into the flour mixture until just combined. Line 24 ½-cup muffin tins with paper cups and divide the batter among them, filling them ⅔ full. Bake for 20 to 25 minutes, or until a tester comes out clean. Invert onto racks to cool. Serve warm or at room temperature. Makes 24 muffins.

CARROT AND RAISIN SWEET ROLLS

These light, sweet rolls are delicious toasted for breakfast.

2 packages active dry yeast
1 ¼ cups warm milk
1 teaspoon sugar
1 cup raisins
1 cup Carrot Puree (p. 28)
½ cup firmly packed light-brown
   sugar
1 stick (½ cup) unsalted butter,
   melted and cooled
1 large egg, beaten lightly

1 tablespoon grated orange peel
1 ½ teaspoons salt
1 ½ teaspoons cinnamon
½ teaspoon freshly grated
   nutmeg
½ teaspoon ground ginger
7 to 8 cups all-purpose flour
Eggwash glaze made by beating
   1 large egg with 1 teaspoon
   water and a pinch of salt

In a large bowl, proof the yeast in ¼ cup of the milk with the sugar for 15 minutes, or until foamy. Meanwhile, in a bowl combine the remaining warm milk with the raisins and let cool.

In a bowl, combine the Carrot Puree, brown sugar, butter, egg, orange peel, salt, spices, and milk and raisin mixture. Add the carrot mixture to the yeast. Stir in the flour, 1 cup at a time, until a soft dough forms. Knead on a floured surface, incorporating more flour if necessary, for 8 to 10 minutes, or until smooth. Put the dough in an oiled bowl, turn it to coat it with the oil, and cover the bowl with plastic wrap and a towel. Let the dough rise for 1½ hours, or until doubled in bulk.

Punch the dough down, knead lightly, and divide in half. Roll each half into a rope 24 inches long and cut each rope into 12 pieces. Form each piece into a ball, arrange about 2 inches apart on oiled baking sheets, and let rise, covered loosely, for 30 to 45 minutes, or until doubled in bulk. Preheat oven to 375° F. Brush rolls with the glaze and bake for 12 to 15 minutes, or until the rolls sound hollow when tapped. Let cool on racks. Makes 24.

THE BIG CARROT BOOK

CARROT SCONES

....

A twist on a classic recipe. Instead of the traditional accompaniments of raspberry jam and Devonshire (clotted) cream, serve these scones with softened butter and orange marmalade.

2 cups all-purpose flour
¼ cup sugar
1 tablespoon baking powder
½ teaspoon baking soda
½ teaspoon cinnamon
¼ teaspoon allspice
¼ teaspoon salt
4 tablespoons cold butter, cut
  into small bits

1 cup Carrot Puree (p. 28)
¼ cup sour cream
3 tablespoons milk or water, if
  needed
Eggwash glaze made by beating
  1 large egg with 1 teaspoon
  water and a pinch of salt

Preheat oven to 425° F.

Into a bowl, sift together the flour, sugar, baking powder, baking soda, cinnamon, allspice, and salt. Rub in the butter until the mixture resembles coarse meal. In another bowl, stir together the Carrot Puree and sour cream. Add the carrot mixture to the flour mixture, and stir, adding additional milk if needed, to form a soft but still slightly sticky dough. Knead the dough lightly on a floured surface for 1 minute and pat it into a ½-inch thick round. Transfer the round to a greased baking sheet, brush with the eggwash glaze, and cut into 8 pie-shaped wedges. Bake for 15 to 20 minutes, or until golden. Serve warm. Makes 8 scones.

DESSERTS

CARROT CELEBRATION CAKE

A wonderful children's birthday cake, although I know many grownups who would greatly appreciate this special treat.

FOR THE CAKE:
2 cups all-purpose flour
1 cup granulated sugar
⅔ cup firmly packed light-brown
   sugar
2 teaspoons baking soda
1 teaspoon salt
2½ teaspoons cinnamon
½ teaspoon freshly grated
   nutmeg
Pinch of ground cloves
4 large eggs
1 cup vegetable oil
4 cups finely grated carrots

2 teaspoons grated orange peel
½ cup sweet orange marmalade
   for filling

FOR THE CREAM CHEESE
FROSTING:
1 pound cream cheese, softened
1 stick (½ cup) unsalted butter,
   softened
4 cups confectioners' sugar,
   sifted
2½ teaspoons vanilla

MAKE THE CAKE: Preheat the oven to 350° F.

Line three 8-inch round cake pans with wax paper and butter the paper. Dust the pans with flour, shaking out the excess.

Sift the flour, sugars, baking soda, salt, cinnamon, nutmeg, and cloves into a bowl. In a large bowl, beat the eggs with an electric mixer. Beat in the oil, and add the flour mixture a little at a time, beating until smooth. Fold in the carrots and orange peel. Divide the batter among the cake pans and bake for 25 to 30 minutes, or until a cake tester comes out clean. Let the layers cool in the pans on racks for 5 minutes. Invert the layers onto the racks and let cool completely. Peel off the wax paper.

Arrange one cake layer on a serving plate, spread half the marmalade over it and top with another cake layer. Spread the second layer with the remaining marmalade and top with the remaining cake layer.

MAKE THE FROSTING: In a large bowl, beat together the cream cheese and butter with an electric mixer until combined well. Add the confectioners' sugar, a little at a time, and beat until fluffy. Beat in the vanilla. Spread the frosting over the sides and top of the cake.

CARROT TART WITH CRYSTALLIZED GINGER

Try this carrot tart, delicately perfumed with ginger, for the holidays instead of the traditional pumpkin pie.

FOR THE NUT CRUST:
1 cup all-purpose flour
⅓ cup finely ground blanched almonds
6 tablespoons cold butter, cut into bits
2 tablespoons cold vegetable shortening
1 teaspoon grated orange peel
1 tablespoon brown sugar
Pinch of salt
2 tablespoons ice water

FOR THE FILLING:
1 recipe Carrot Puree (p. 28)
2 large eggs, lightly beaten
⅓ cup firmly packed light-brown sugar
1 cup heavy or light cream
2 tablespoons finely minced crystallized ginger
1 teaspoon cinnamon
¼ teaspoon freshly grated nutmeg
2 teaspoons grated orange peel

MAKE THE CRUST: In a large bowl, mix the flour, nuts, butter, shortening, orange peel, sugar, and salt together with a pastry blender. Add the ice water and toss the mixture until it forms a dough, adding additional water if necessary. Knead the dough lightly, form it into a ball, wrap in plastic, and chill for 1 hour.

Preheat the oven to 350° F.

Roll out the pastry ⅛-inch thick and fit it into a 9-inch tart pan with a removable rim. Prick the bottom of the shell with a fork and chill for 30 minutes. Line the shell with wax paper and bake for 10 to 12 minutes, until pale golden in color. Let cool in the pan on a rack.

TO MAKE THE FILLING: In a bowl, whisk together the Carrot Puree, eggs, sugar, cream, ginger, spices, and orange peel until smooth. Pour the filling into the shell and bake for 30 minutes, or until a knife comes out clean. Serve the tart warm or at room temperature. Serves 8.

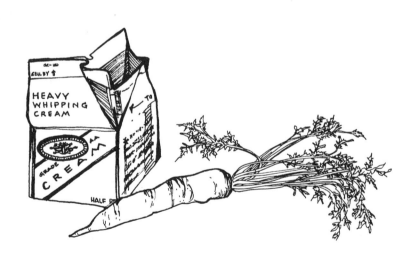

BROWN SUGAR CARROT PUDDING

....

This is pure comfort food, made elegant by the addition of whipped cream or a custard sauce.

1 stick (½ cup) butter, softened
1½ cups firmly packed light-
  brown sugar
3 large eggs
2 tablespoons lemon juice
2 teaspoons grated lemon peel
1 cup all-purpose flour

1 teaspoon baking powder
½ teaspoon baking soda
½ teaspoon salt
1 teaspoon cinnamon
¼ teaspoon ground allspice
1½ cups finely grated carrots

Preheat the oven to 350° F.

In a large bowl with an electric mixer, cream the butter with the sugar until light and fluffy. Beat in the eggs, 1 at a time, the lemon juice and grated peel. Sift the flour, baking powder, baking soda, salt, cinnamon, and allspice and stir into the butter mixture. Fold in the carrots. Transfer the batter to a buttered 1½-quart shallow baking dish and cover it with buttered foil.

Set the baking dish into a baking pan, adding enough hot water to reach halfway up the sides of the dish. Bake the pudding for 30 minutes. Remove the foil and bake for 30 minutes more, or until a cake tester comes out clean. Serve the pudding warm with lightly whipped cream or a custard sauce. Serves 6–8.

SPICED CARROT CUPCAKES

These lovely little cupcakes are perfect for school holidays and birthdays. Simply sprinkle with confectioners' sugar or use the Cream Cheese Frosting from the Carrot Celebration Cake recipe (p. 85).

1 ⅓ cups sifted all-purpose flour
1 ½ teaspoons baking powder
¾ teaspoon baking soda
1 ½ teaspoons cinnamon
½ teaspoon ginger
¼ teaspoon nutmeg

2 large eggs
1 ¼ cups sugar
½ cup vegetable oil
1 recipe Carrot Puree (p. 28)
Confectioners' sugar for garnish

Preheat the oven to 325° F.

Into a bowl, sift the flour, baking powder, soda, and spices. In another bowl, whisk together the eggs, sugar, vegetable oil, and Carrot Puree. Gradually add the dry ingredients to the carrot mixture. Spoon the batter into 12 buttered muffin pans, filling them ⅔ full.

Bake the cupcakes for 25 to 30 minutes, or until a cake tester comes out clean. Let the cupcakes cool in the pan on a rack for 5 minutes, invert them onto the rack and let them cool completely. Before serving, sift the confectioners' sugar over the tops of the cupcakes, if desired. Makes 12 cupcakes.

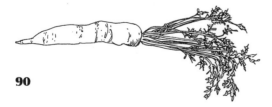

THE BIG CARROT BOOK

INDEX

· · · · · · · · · ·

Sauces:
  chive cream, 26
  cucumber dill, 19
  dilled mustard, 53
  fennel-scented carrot,
    49–50
  peanut, 38–39
Scallion, carrot, and potato
  fritters, 20
Scones, carrot, 81
Shrimp, julienned carrot,
    snowpea, and red pep-
    per salad with toasted
    sesame seeds and, 36–37
Side dishes, 61–73
  carrot, leek, and potato
    gratin, 66
  carrot puree, 28
  carrots baked in mustard
    cream sauce, 64
  carrots with basil oil and
    mint, 70
  carrot timbales, 67
  creamed baby carrots with
    dill, 73
  glazed carrots and turnips,
    65
  orange-gingered carrots,
    63

roasted carrot and apple
  puree, 72
sautéed carrots, pearl
  onions, and brussels
  sprouts in lemon butter,
  68
sautéed carrots with garlic,
  black olives, and parsley,
  69
see also Salads
Slaw, carrot, red cabbage,
  and Roquefort, with
  walnuts, 34
Snacks, see Appetizers and
  snacks
Snowpea, julienned carrot,
  red pepper and, salad
  with shrimp and toasted
  sesame seeds, 36–37
Soups, 9–14
  carrot, leek, and potato,
    12
  creamy carrot and white
    turnip, 14
  gingered carrot, 11
  iced carrot and orange, 13
Spiced:
  carrot and apricot muffins,
    78

carrot cupcakes, 90
Spinach, carrot, and white
  radish salad, 35
Sweet rolls, carrot and raisin,
  79–80

Tarts:
  carrot, leek, and celery, 24
  carrot, with crystallized
    ginger, 87–88
Timbales, carrot, 67
Tofu, carrot, and rice casserole with toasted
  almonds, 59
Turnip(s):
  glazed carrots and, 65
  white, and carrot soup,
    creamy, 14

Walnut(s):
  carrot, and mushroom
    pâté, 17–18
  carrot, red cabbage, and
    Roquefort slaw with, 34

Yogurt:
  carrot, and cucumber
    salad, Indian-style, 40
  cream, dilled, 27

ABOUT THE AUTHOR

GEORGIA DOWNARD, a writer and former food editor at *Gourmet* magazine, is a food stylist and teacher. She currently works for the Television Food Network as its Culinary Director. She lives in New York City with her two children.

ABOUT THE TYPE

This book was set in Sabon, a typeface designed by the well-known German typographer Jan Tschichold (1902–74). Sabon's design is based upon the original letter forms of Claude Garamond and was created specifically to be used for three sources: foundry type for hand composition, Linotype, and Monotype. Tschichold named his typeface for the famous Frankfurt typefounder Jacques Sabon, who died in 1580.